BIRD *and*
FLOWER EMBLEMS
of the United States

BIRD *and*
FLOWER EMBLEMS
of the United States

Hilda Simon

DODD, MEAD & COMPANY · NEW YORK

Library of Congress Cataloging in Publication Data

Simon, Hilda.
    Bird and flower emblems of the United States.

    Includes index.
    SUMMARY: Text and illustrations introduce the
bird and flower emblems of all fifty of
the United States.
    1. State birds—Juvenile literature—Pictorial
works. 2. State flowers—Juvenile literature—
Pictorial works. [1. State birds. 2. State
flowers. 3. Emblems, State] I. Title.
QL682.S55   598.2′973   78-7324
ISBN 0-396-07581-9

CONTENTS

BIRD *and*
FLOWER EMBLEMS
of the United States

BIRDS AND FLOWERS
AS EMBLEMS

An Introduction

Throughout mankind's history, people have used a variety of animals and plants as symbols for ideas and concepts ranging from the religious to the political. Very often, the special significance of such a plant or animal was confined to a single people or culture; others, however, had almost universal appeal that reached across national borders and individual cultures. Thus the date palm frond, the ancient Jewish symbol of victory that was spread before Jesus during His triumphant entry into Jerusalem, was chosen because this palm was a valuable and cherished tree in the Middle East, and because its leaves remained green throughout the year. But to the peoples of Northern Europe, this exotic—and in their countries all but unknown—tree could have no such meaning; although palm fronds continued to play a role in Christian religious customs on Palm Sunday, the original significance of the tree and its evergreen leaf was obscured. On the other hand, symbols of strength and power such as the eagle and falcon were easily appreciated in many different countries because large birds of prey are common all over the world.

In the past, many of the animal and plant emblems selected had religious connotations. Fear and awe of animal strength and power, admiration of special beauty or unusual characteristics, as well as the vital importance of certain plants and animals, often moved ancient peoples to include them in their mythology and assign symbolical significance to them. In more recent times, the importance of religious symbolism declined, yet even modern countries often turn to the plant and animal kingdoms for selection of suitable emblems, birds and flowers being obvious favorites.

Usually, the plant or animal chosen means something very special to that particular region or country; in that respect, not much has changed over the centuries. Rather surprisingly, however, economic importance seems to

The strange, flightless kiwi.

The long-plumed quetzal of Central America.

have had a very small part in the selection of most emblems. Thus, New Zealand made the unique and rare flightless kiwi its national bird, displaying it on the country's great seal, on postage stamps, and on many of its products; the members of New Zealand's armed forces proudly call themselves "kiwis." Similarly, Guatemalans chose the quetzal, the sacred bird of the ancient Aztecs, as their national emblem, and display it just as proudly on their seal and their stamps; even the Guatemalan monetary unit is called a quetzal. And indeed, this member of the small trogon family is worthy of such honor, being a breathtakingly beautiful bird whose soft gleaming plumes show a variety of rainbow hues ranging from pure emerald green to a deep violet blue.

The choice of such birds as the kiwi and the quetzal are easy to understand for us; many of the choices by ancient peoples remain more obscure. Thus, the bird known even today as the sacred ibis was truly sacred to the Egyptians, as testified to by the many carefully preserved ibis mummies found in old Egyptian graves. The bird was the symbol of their god Thoth, the scribe of the gods, who is often depicted as having the head of an ibis. The reasons for so honoring this bird are not known for certain, although it has been suggested that the appearance of ibises in numbers may have heralded the periodical floodings of Egyptian agricultural lands by the Nile waters. Since the economic welfare of the people in that arid region depended largely on such floodings, the Nile river was a god to the Egyptians, and the bird which by its arrival foretold the rise of the waters could well have been considered a messenger of the gods. A practical people, the ancient Egyptians usually did not venerate any animal without what to them was a good and sufficient reason.

The sacred ibis of the Egyptians.

Ancient symbol of power: the golden eagle.

Ancient Rome chose the eagle—more accurately, the golden eagle—as the symbol of its might and power. Engraved on the Roman standards, it was introduced into all regions conquered by that empire. But even without Rome's intervention, eagles and the closely related falcons were obvious symbols of power and strength, and became favored heraldic birds, especially during Europe's Age of Chivalry when hunting with the help of trained falcons reached its peak there. The strength, grace, and magnificent flying powers of these feathered predators deeply impressed the humans who observed and used them without ever being able to really tame them. Even as the lion was considered the King of the Beasts, so the eagle was acknowledged as the undisputed King of the Air. As a consequence, most royal houses featured one or the other of these animals in their coats of arms; the eagle seems to have been a special favorite.

The choice of large birds of prey as symbols of power and nobility is understandable. A good deal more difficult to appreciate are the reasons that led to the selection of, among all birds, the dove as the visual embodiment of the Holy Ghost, the third part of the Trinity. Even though the dove in question was white, and the color undoubtedly played a part, there were many other white birds—some much more impressive—that could have fulfilled that particular requirement. Perhaps, however, a look at some natural history facts about the rock dove —usually known today as the domestic pigeon—can shed some light on the mystery.

Normally a bluish-gray color in the wild, rock doves are native to the Middle East as well as parts of Africa and Asia. Distinguished from others of their kind by a preference for steep rocks and sheer cliffsides as breeding sites, these wild birds were more or less predestined to living near human beings and eventually becoming domesticated. When men began to erect tall buildings of stone, the doves quickly took possession of these convenient artificial cliffsides, and easily adapted to the necessary presence of human beings. Since the tallest and most imposing structures erected by the ancients were the tem-

White variety of the rock dove.

ples built for their deities, the birds that flocked around them soon became associated with these sacred places in the minds of the people.

There are indications that at least some of the ancient Middle Eastern peoples kept and protected rock doves without, however, using them for food. In such a sheltered existence, the rare, conspicuous white variants, which in the wild were quickly eliminated by natural enemies, could not only survive, but also could reproduce and pass on their color—or rather lack of color—to their offspring. Such a pure white bird, circling the temples on silent wings, could then well be seen as an unearthly creature, and even as the embodiment of the Holy Spirit come down from above during so special an occurrence as the baptism of Jesus. True to tradition, religious art has depicted the Holy Ghost as a white dove throughout the history of Christianity. Yet this bird had other ancient connotations: the feathered messenger returning to Noah with the olive branch that signaled the end of the Great Flood was a dove, and in some old pagan cultures, the bird was regarded as the symbol of gentleness and sensual love. In time, a combination of these various concepts produced the universally accepted symbol of the "peace dove." Shown holding an olive branch—itself a time-honored peace offering—in its bill, the dove was adopted as the emblem of peace by the United Nations.

Just as the olive branch has signified peaceful intentions since ancient times, so laurel leaves have for ages been the symbol of victory, honor, and fame, ever since the Greeks began to give a laurel wreath, or crown, to the winners in the Pythian games, which were held every four years in Delphi in honor of that town's patron god Apollo.

Among flowers, the rose was one of the earliest favorites of people from many different countries, and was used as an emblem even in the distant past. To the ancient Romans, the rose was the symbol of secrecy and discretion. This is indicated by the old Latin expression *sub rosa*, under the rose, which is still used today to designate

Cultivated roses, especially their red and white varieties, were often used as emblems.

something told in confidence and under circumstances forbidding disclosure. In addition, the beauty, grace, and fragrance of this flower, as well as the sharp thorns that protect it, all played a part in its becoming a favored floral emblem for a variety of groups and causes in the course of history. Thus, in the fifteenth-century War of the Roses in England, the House of York chose a red rose, and the House of Lancaster a white one, as their respective symbols.

To this day, the rose is England's floral emblem; in the United States, it was the choice of the District of Columbia and four out of the fifty states. The rose was also used frequently to symbolize spiritual and idealistic concepts and causes. The persecuted early Lutheran

Protestants adopted as their emblem a white rose standing for purity, surrounded by thorns signifying Christ's suffering—and, by implication, the suffering of any Christians for their faith. This religious concept and the rose's ancient symbolism of secrecy moved a group of young people in Hitler's Germany to adopt it as their emblem. Compelled by an overwhelming need to raise a voice for morality, right, and decency in a country gone mad under Hitler, the students' group known as the White Rose printed and distributed anti-Nazi leaflets. All of them paid with their lives on the scaffold for their dauntless integrity and courage.

Like the rose, the lily also was often used as an emblem; especially the white-flowered kinds called Madonna and Easter lilies became Christian symbols of purity and spirituality. On the other hand, the heraldic French lily known as *fleur-de-lis* was probably inspired by the iris, rather than by a true lily.

The all-white Madonna lily.

After the founding of our country, the search for a suitable emblem to represent the United States caused much debate. Unlike Canada, which chose the maple leaf, Americans from the beginning favored an animal. The question was, which animal? The choice was not easy; although everyone agreed that it should be a species typical of this country, and preferably not found in Europe, the agreement ended there. Amazingly enough, there was strong early sentiment for a creature many people find not only terrifying but repulsive: the rattlesnake, which was seriously suggested as the national emblem of the new republic. Actually, several Revolutionary flags, including the first naval jack of the young Union, featured the rattlesnake, usually shown in a coiled position, and invariably with the legend "Don't Tread on Me." It is not difficult to understand why the independent-minded fighters of the Revolutionary War saw a parallel between themselves and an animal which attacked only when provoked, but once roused could deliver a deadly blow even to a superior enemy. That the snake was not acceptable to the majority, which did not relish the idea of having the United States represented by a dangerously venomous reptile, is no less understandable.

In the end, Americans, like so many others before them, selected an eagle as their national emblem. A member of a group known as sea eagles rather than the legendary golden eagle, this American species is very inappropriately called the bald eagle, a name which easily conjures up a vulturelike image with a naked head and neck. Nothing could be further from the truth, for the bald eagle's head and neck are thickly covered with feathers that are dark in the immature bird but turn pure white in the adult. Although there are several other kinds of sea eagles in other parts of the world, the bald eagle is found only in America. Congress finally adopted it as our emblem over the protests of Benjamin Franklin, who would have preferred the turkey, which, even though it is neither a graceful nor a majestic-looking bird, is certainly, as Franklin argued, an eminently useful one. Once again, however, usefulness did not rank high as a yardstick employed in choosing an emblem, and the bald eagle, which in appearance is certainly every bit as majestic as its close relative of ancient fame, became the national bird of the young American republic.

Selection of plant and animal emblems by individual states of the Union came very much later; although an early preference for certain flowers was shown in many regions, the first few official designations of state floral emblems were not made until the 1890s. It is interesting to note, however, that some states made their choices official while they were still Territories. Although selection of state birds lagged even more behind, a growing interest in nature generally, and especially in birds after the turn of the century, accelerated the process. Some states of course had their widely accepted favorite birds long before officially designating them as emblems; thus, the California gull was Utah's undisputed front-runner ever since flocks of these birds had saved the pioneers' crops from marauding locusts in the middle of the past century.

Eventually, after the selections had been made by such groups as women's clubs and schoolchildren, every single state of the Union adopted both a flower and a bird as emblems.

This book is essentially a full-color portrait gallery of all the state flowers and birds of the United States, accompanied by short, informative paragraphs. In order to avoid confusion and assure equal treatment for every state, those birds and flowers that were chosen by more than one were repeated for each state, with only minor variations and additions to both text and pictures.

ALABAMA

Camellia 1959 • Yellowhammer 1927

For several decades, the goldenrod was Alabama's state flower but, in 1959, that wildflower was replaced by the camellia, an ornamental shrub with large, waxy white or red blossoms.

The plant belongs to a Far Eastern family of shrubs, many of which are cultivated in order to harvest their leaves and buds which, after curing, are used for the beverage known as tea. The camellia, however, is just an ornamental plant grown for its handsome flowers. It was named after the Jesuit priest Georg Joseph Kamel—usually spelled Camelli—who allegedly brought this plant from the Far East to Europe, where it became a greenhouse shrub.

Among the dozens of vernacular names assigned locally to the yellow-shafted flicker, "yellowhammer" is the one most often used in the South. This woodpecker can be observed searching for ants on the ground, and is easily recognized by its black "mustache" and by the red crescent on the back of its otherwise grayish neck. The yellow lining of the wing and tail feathers usually becomes visible only when the bird takes flight. Like all woodpeckers, flickers are cavity nesters.

The Alabama legislature designated the yellowhammer as the state bird in 1927. Among the reasons advanced for the choice were the bird's predominant colors, which supposedly suggest the gray, yellow-trimmed uniforms of the Confederate cavalry.

ALASKA

Forget-me-not 1917 • Willow Ptarmigan 1955

Forget-me-nots are a widespread group of small, white-
or blue-flowered herbs. One of the blue varieties has been
traditionally acknowledged as the symbol of fidelity and
friendship in many countries, and has found a place in
numerous old songs and stories. Although the species
adopted by Alaska as its floral emblem is not the common
forget-me-not of European fame, it is a close alpine relative, and has similar bright blue flowers. Forget-me-not
blue is an accepted color description, specified as a blue-
green blue of medium brilliance.

Alaska designated the forget-me-not as its state
flower in 1917 while still a Territory.

A bird of the extreme northern latitudes, the willow
ptarmigan is often used as a model to illustrate adaptive

coloration among some animals living in snowbound regions. Largely a mottled brown in summer, this arctic grouse, along with its smaller relatives, the white-tailed and rock ptarmigans, changes into a pure white feather dress in winter. All of these small grouse live in an environment of bleak tundra and arctic mountain slopes where few other birds could survive. The willow ptarmigan's popular name refers to that grouse's preference for willow scrub in sheltered valleys during wintertime. The nest is a grass- and feather-lined hollow on the tundra.

The ptarmigan was officially adopted as Alaska's state bird in 1955.

ARIZONA

Saguaro Blossom 1931 • Cactus Wren 1931

The saguaro, or giant cactus, of the Southwest may grow to a height of sixty feet. Found only in the deserts of Arizona and parts of Mexico, this huge arborescent cactus is a distinctive-looking plant. When in bloom, the tall columnar, often sparsely branched trunks bear at their tips beautiful cream-colored waxy flowers that ripen into edible fruit. The name is of Pima Indian origin, and the Indians have many old tales about this cactus, which they believed to possess great curative powers.

The saguaro blossom was adopted as a floral emblem by the Territory of Arizona in 1901, and officially confirmed as the state flower in 1931 by legislative action.

26

The heavily spotted cactus wren is the giant among the North American species of this New World group of birds. All the old European folktales about the wren refer to the only member of this family found outside the Western Hemisphere, and known in this country as the winter wren. The ten North American species range in size from the tiny four-inch winter wren to the cactus wren, which is more than twice as long. Stands of yucca, cactus, mesquite, and other desert vegetation are favored by this wren. There, surrounded by spines and thorns that furnish natural protection, it builds its football-shaped nest which features a side entrance.

The cactus wren was officially designated as the state bird of Arizona by legislative action in 1931.

ARKANSAS

Apple Blossom 1901 • Mockingbird 1929

By choosing the apple blossom as their floral emblem, two of our states have paid homage to one of the oldest, most famous, and most widely distributed fruits trees in the world. The apple blossom was adopted as Arkansas' state flower by an act of its legislature in 1901.

There are probably few other sights better suited to bring to mind so vividly the feeling of spring in temperate zones as the spectacle of an apple orchard in full bloom. As bees hum about in the scented air, the branches with their tightly packed, delicate pink-and-white blossoms provide not only beauty for the eye, but also the promise of a rich harvest of delicious fruit later on in the year.

The mockingbird was designated as the state bird of Arkansas by an act of legislation in 1929. More than perhaps any other, the mockingbird is considered the favorite among American songbirds, which accounts for the fact that five states in all have selected it as their emblem.

Famed as an accomplished vocalist, the mockingbird is unique in that its repertoire includes a great many songs of other birds in often perfect imitations, and also various notes, sounds, and noises picked up from its environment.

Mockingbirds occur throughout the entire southern half of the country, but are most numerous in the South and Southwest. They like to stay around human habitations and often build their rootlet-lined cup of a nest in gardens near houses. Not the least bit shy, they like to tease the family dog or cat.

CALIFORNIA

California Poppy 1903 • California Quail 1931

One of the best-known western flowers, the California, or golden, poppy can be found in abundance in the valleys and foothills of the Pacific Coast, as well as in parts of the Rockies. Large areas may be carpeted with the orange-golden flowers that open by day but close at night.

Although they belong to the family which includes the famous opium poppy, none of the American species contain the narcotic drug of their Old World relatives. Cultivated varieties of the golden poppy may have cream, pink, and even white blossoms. An act of the California state legislature adopted the California poppy as the floral emblem in 1903.

Attractively colored and patterned, friendly and gregarious, the California quail, or California valley quail, is

30

without a doubt one of the most charming of the smaller grouse-like birds. A hundred years ago, the French naturalist Coues, who traveled in the Southwest, described this quail and its close relatives in almost lyrical terms, calling them "beautiful to the eye and to the heart . . . birds that win friends by the charms of their personality . . ."

It is fortunate that the California quail adapted well to man's presence; flocks of semi-tame birds may be seen in the parks of several western cities. Wild birds are still common in uninhabited or sparsely inhabited areas, including desert regions. The California legislature confirmed the California quail as the state bird in 1931.

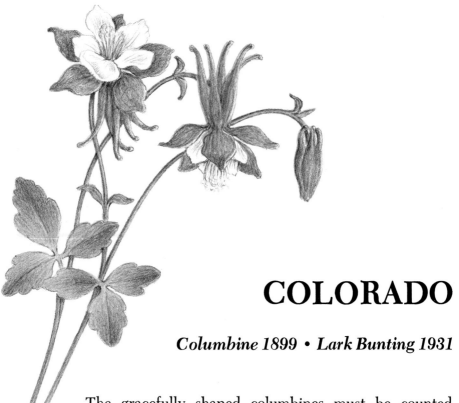

COLORADO

Columbine 1899 • Lark Bunting 1931

The gracefully shaped columbines must be counted
among the most attractive of all our wildflowers. They
come in a variety of colors. The most common eastern
kind has scarlet and yellow blossoms, but there also are
all-yellow, white, and blue columbines. Colorado chose
as its floral emblem the delicate pale blue—or rather
white and lavender—variety known as the Rocky Mountain columbine.

The name of these perennials stems from the
imagined—and rather far-fetched—resemblance of the
flower to a group of five doves, from *columba*, the Latin
word for dove. Designated as state flower of Colorado by
the legislature in 1899, the blue columbine received protection under the law by an act passed in 1925.

32

Native to the western plains and prairies, lark buntings are inconspicuous birds during wintertime, when both males and females wear a brownish, striped, sparrowlike feather dress. In spring, however, the male changes into its breeding plumage, which is overall velvety black offset by large white wing patches. Like the rest of its group, which includes the finches and sparrows, the lark bunting feeds on seeds, grains, and insects. The nest is a loose cup built on the ground, and resembles that of many ground-nesting sparrows. The pleasant song, often heard on the wing, includes many clear piping and trilling sounds.

The lark bunting was designated as state bird by an act of the Colorado legislature in 1931.

CONNECTICUT

Mountain Laurel 1907 • Robin 1943

An evergreen American shrub, the mountain laurel brings forth its beautiful clusters of small, rose-colored or pinkish-white flowers in late spring. Adopted by two eastern states as their floral emblem, this handsome shrub is not closely related to the true laurel of Europe, which since ancient times has been the symbol of honor, fame, and victory. The leaves of the mountain laurel, which belongs in the azalea and rhododendron group, are poisonous when eaten.

In 1907, the legislature of Connecticut adopted the mountain laurel as the state flower. Among the reasons advanced for the choice were "the beauty of its blossoms and foliage, its sturdy and abundant growth in the state, and its general popularity."

In 1943, the robin was officially designated as Connecticut's state bird. Two other states have also named it as their favorite.

Welcomed as the unerring harbinger of spring in many parts of the United States, the robin is a cheerful, friendly bird whose pleasant song enlivens many a suburban backyard and garden. It builds its mud-walled, grass-lined nest in a tree often close to human habitations.

The American robin was so named by homesick English settlers because it reminded them of the gentle "Robin Redbreast" of their homeland. The European robin, however, is a much smaller, warblerlike bird not closely related to the American species, which is a true thrush.

DELAWARE

Peach Blossom 1895 • *Blue Hen Chicken 1939*

By common popular consent, the peach blossom was chosen as Delaware's floral emblem because of that state's supremacy in peach growing, and was officially adopted in 1895. The delicate pink blossoms of this tree appear on twigs whose leaves are still only buds.

Peach is an accepted color description of a delicate, somewhat yellowish pink. The tree's name comes from the French "peche," which in turn is a corruption of the Latin *persica*, for this exotic fruit was widely known as "Persian apple" in the past.

By choosing the "Blue Hen Chicken" as its state bird, Delaware immortalized a tradition that goes back to the Revolutionary War. At that time, soldiers from Delaware took along gamecocks said to be superior to other fighting cocks because they were the offspring of a certain famous blue hen. The story of these cockfights spread through the army, and when the men from Delaware showed exemplary bravery in battle, they were nicknamed "Blue Hen's Chickens."

Throughout the years, the legendary fighting cocks received unofficial recognition in Delaware by being used as a motif for political campaigns, for publications, and as mascots. In 1939, the "Blue Hen Chicken" was officially designated as Delaware's state bird.

FLORIDA

Orange Blossom 1909 • Mockingbird 1907

Florida's extensive citrus industry would have made the orange blossom a logical choice for the "land of the Flowers," even if this long-standing symbol of marriage were not so attractive and fragrant a flower.

The orange, which originally hails from Asia, was established in the United States as an economically valuable fruit tree during the first half of the nineteenth century, and has become one of our country's all-time favorite fruits. The name evolved in a series of changes from the Sanskrit *naranga* through Persian, Arabic, and French word usage.

The Florida state legislature officially adopted the orange blossom in 1909.

The first of five states to select the mockingbird as its emblem in 1907, Florida thereby proclaimed its preference for what is considered the favorite among American songbirds. The Florida legislative act adopting this "bird of matchless charm" cited among the reasons for the choice the "melody of its music that delights the heart."

Famed as an accomplished vocalist, the mockingbird is unique in that its repertoire includes a great many songs of other birds in often perfect imitations, and also various notes, sounds, and noises picked up from its environment.

Mockingbirds occur throughout the entire southern half of the country, but are most numerous in the South and Southwest. They like to stay around human habitations and often build their rootlet-lined cup of a nest in gardens near houses. Not the least bit shy, they like to tease the family dog or cat.

GEORGIA

Cherokee Rose 1916 • Brown Thrasher 1935

The climbing Cherokee rose is found widely throughout the state of Georgia, and is often used to form hedges. It may have been introduced directly to the state from China, or by way of England around 1760. The Cherokee Indians widely distributed the plant, which accounts for its popular name. It not only blooms regularly every spring, but sometimes also in the fall. Its waxy-white flowers have petals of a wonderfully velvety texture.

The Cherokee rose was declared the state floral emblem by the Georgia House of Representatives in 1916. Among the reasons given was the fact that the rose "grows with equal luxuriance in every county of the State."

A fine songster that rivals the mockingbird in musical talents but makes no attempt to mimic other birds' songs, the brown thrasher is the only one among the eight North American members of this group that occurs in the East. Its rich chestnut coloring and long tail make this bird easy to identify.

Not as tame as its close relatives, the mockingbirds and catbirds, the thrasher usually likes to keep its home at a distance from human habitations, and is known to frequent wilder, noninhabited areas. Its nest is a twiggy, cuplike structure built in a dense bush, usually near the ground.

Schoolchildren selected the brown thrasher in 1928 as the best candidate for the state bird, and it was officially adopted in 1935.

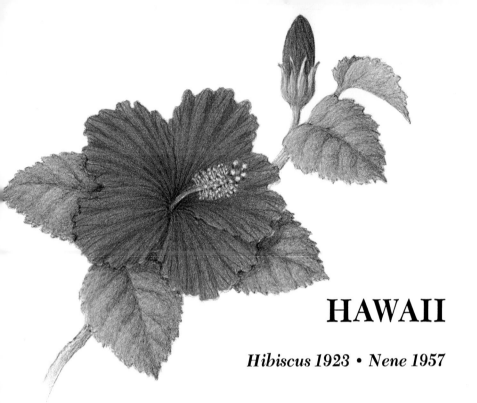

HAWAII

Hibiscus 1923 • Nene 1957

Until 1923, the beautiful red, powderpuff-shaped blossom of the native lehua tree was considered Hawaii's state flower. In that year, however, it was replaced by the hibiscus blossom. Members of the rose mallow group, which includes numerous herbs, shrubs, and small trees with showy flowers in a variety of colors, different species of hibiscus are common, especially in many of the warmer regions of the world.

The often treelike shrub popularly called the Rose of Sharon is one of the best-known hibiscus varieties, and is a favorite ornamental.

A unique Hawaiian goose, the nene was close to extinction just a few decades ago. Out of a population believed to have numbered about 25,000 before man came to the islands, only some thirty wild birds survived.

At home in the upland lava areas, the nene has only partially webbed feet, is a poor swimmer, and feeds largely on land. It fell an easy prey to overhunting and the depredations of dogs and other predators introduced by man to the islands. Attempts at restocking the wild population by breeding these geese in captivity, and then releasing them in their native habitats on the islands of Maui and Hawaii, apparently have been successful.

In 1957, the people of Hawaii adopted this unusual goose as their state bird.

IDAHO

Syringa 1931 • Mountain Bluebird 1931

Often called "mock orange," the American shrub known popularly as syringa should not be confused with the European shrub that can also lay claim to that name but is more commonly called lilac. The latter belongs in the olive family. The American syringa, on the other hand, is a member of the Hydrangeaceae, a large group of flowering shrubs, many of which—such as the widely-grown hydrangea, from which the family takes its name—are favorite ornamentals in parks and gardens.

Although affectionately known as the Idaho state flower since 1893, the syringa did not officially receive that title until 1931, when it was so designated by the state legislature.

The mountain bluebird was officially named as the Idaho state bird by the legislature in 1931. Two of our western states chose it as their favorite.

The bluebird of the western mountain ranges lacks the rust-colored breast of its close relative, the common bluebird of the East and West. Instead, this small thrush is overall turquoise blue, somewhat paler below, and with a whitish belly. Its song is a short, clear warble.

Open terrain with scattered trees is the mountain bluebird's preferred environment, but it sometimes will live around farms, very much like its relatives. Also like other bluebirds, it is a cavity nester, and may be willing to accept a bird box as a substitute for the hole in a dead tree or stump in which it normally would build its nest.

ILLINOIS

Violet 1908 • Cardinal 1929

One of the best known and best loved of all small wild-flowers, the violet was chosen by four states as their floral emblem. Although it was declared the state flower by the Illinois legislature in 1903, the law so designating it did not go into effect until 1908.

Long the symbol of modesty and shyness, violets are widely distributed in both the Old and New Worlds. Of the more than 300 species found worldwide, about 100 occur in the United States. In addition to the familiar blue violets, there are white and even yellow-flowered kinds. The latter include the downy yellow violet, which may grow to a height of eighteen inches.

The Illinois legislature designated the cardinal as the state bird in 1929. No fewer than seven states have selected this beautiful bird as their emblem.

Easily identified because both the bright red male and the duller, brownish female wear crests, the cardinal is further distinguished by the fact that the male keeps its colorful plumage throughout the entire year.

In wintertime, when snow is on the ground, cardinals provide flashes of brilliant scarlet as they visit bird feeders for their favorite sunflower seeds. Originally a bird of river thickets and woodland edges, the cardinal has adapted well to man's presence, and now makes its home in suburban areas and even in towns, where it is a welcome guest. Its nest is a loose cup built in a bush or thicket.

INDIANA

Peony 1957 • Cardinal 1933

Adoption of the peony as Indiana's floral emblem was that state's fourth choice since 1913 when the carnation was selected. A few years later, the carnation was replaced by the flower of the tulip tree, and in 1931, Indiana's General Assembly officially designated the common zinnia as the state flower, thereby repealing the earlier law. In 1957, the zinnia was replaced by the peony.

Favorite garden plants because of their large, showy white, pink, or red flowers, peonies belong to the crowfoot family, whose most familiar wild-growing members are the buttercups.

One of seven states that selected the cardinal as their state bird, Indiana confirmed its choice by an act of legislature in 1933.

48

Easily identified because both the bright red male and the duller, brownish female wear crests, the cardinal is further distinguished by the fact that the male keeps its colorful plumage throughout the entire year.

In wintertime, when snow is on the ground, cardinals provide flashes of brilliant scarlet as they visit bird feeders for their favorite sunflower seeds. Originally a bird of river thickets and woodland edges, the cardinal has adapted well to man's presence, and now makes its home in suburban areas and even in towns, where it is a welcome guest. Its nest is a loose cup built in a bush or thicket.

IOWA

Wild Rose 1897 • American Goldfinch 1933

The wild rose was adopted as the state flower by an act of the Iowa General Assembly in 1897. The perennial favorite of poets and songwriters, the wild rose has been selected by three states as their floral emblem.

The fragrant, delicate pink or white blossoms of these rambling shrubs long ago captured the affection and imagination of people in many countries. Roses probably were among the earliest of cultivated flowers, and are mentioned in some very ancient literature. As noted in the introduction, the rose was in the past considered a symbol of discretion and secrecy, and frequently used as an emblem.

In 1933, the Iowa legislature adopted the American goldfinch—also known as the common or eastern goldfinch—thereby confirming the earlier choice of the Iowa Ornithological Union. The male, in its breeding plumage, is one of our most attractive smaller birds, which perhaps is why two states chose this bird.

During wintertime, both males and females wear a rather drab grayish-green feather dress, but in spring the males change to bright yellow set off by black wings and tail, and a black forehead.

These birds live in open, weedy fields and travel in flocks. They often can be seen clinging to the stem of a tall weed or grass while picking off the seeds. The nest is a tightly woven feltlike cup placed in a bush or tree.

KANSAS

Sunflower 1903 • Western Meadowlark 1937

For the floral emblem of a prairie state, there could be few better choices than a sunflower, for these large-flowered plants, as their name implies, prefer open, sunny locations. Of the more than sixty different kinds of sunflowers found in this country, almost two-thirds grow west of the Rockies. The common sunflower chosen as the Kansas floral emblem is not only the tallest but also the one with the largest flower disk.

The legislative act designating it as the state flower of Kansas declares that, among other things, the sunflower "has to all Kansans a historic symbolism which speaks of frontier days, winding trails, pathless prairies, and is full of the life and glory of the past . . ."

52

The western meadowlark was adopted as the Kansas state bird in 1937, making Kansas one of six states to select this common and attractive bird of the open prairies as its emblem.

The meadowlark's song is clear and pleasant, but that of the western species is much more musical than that of the otherwise very similar eastern kind.

Members of the blackbird and oriole group, and not closely related to the true larks, meadowlarks are cherished because of their beauty, their song, and their value as checks on pest insects. The seeds they also eat are largely from noncultivated grasses and weeds. The nest is a grassy, partially domed cup built on the ground.

KENTUCKY

Goldenrod 1926 • Cardinal 1926

The General Assembly of the Commonwealth of Kentucky officially designated the goldenrod as the state floral emblem in 1926. Two states have selected this wildflower, which is abundant throughout the country.

Of the more than 120 kinds of goldenrod in the United States, a few have pale yellow or even white flowers, but the great majority display the typical golden yellow that gave the plants their name.

Goldenrods bloom from summer to fall, and may line roadsides or carpet acres of meadows with a sheet of bright golden color. A few species have adapted to life in marshes, sandy beaches, deserts, and mountains, so that some kinds of goldenrods can be found in almost every part of the country.

In the same year that it selected its state flower, 1926, Kentucky became one of seven states to make the cardinal its choice for state bird.

Easily identified because both the bright red male and the duller, brownish female wear crests, the cardinal is further distinguished by the fact that the male keeps its colorful plumage throughout the entire year.

In wintertime, when snow is on the ground, cardinals provide flashes of brilliant scarlet as they visit bird feeders for their favorite sunflower seeds. Originally a bird of river thickets and woodland edges, the cardinal has adapted well to man's presence, and now makes its home in suburban areas and even in towns. Its nest is a loose cup built in a bush or thicket.

LOUISIANA

Magnolia 1900 • Brown Pelican

Louisiana designated the evergreen magnolia as the state's floral emblem in 1900 by legislative action. No other flower personifies better the atmosphere and legendary charm of the Old South than the large, fragrant, white or pink blossoms of *Magnolia grandiflora*, the evergreen magnolia. Two states have adopted it as their emblem.

Magnolias were named after French botanist Pierre Magnol (1638-1715). They comprise a group of trees and shrubs with large, showy blossoms that may range in color from white to pink and purple.

The brown pelican is one of the two species of these birds found in North America, and the only dark-colored among the six kinds that are known worldwide. In this

56

country, brown pelicans occur only along the southern Atlantic coast.

In antiquity, these birds were renowned for their alleged habit of sacrificing themselves for their young by piercing their breasts so the nestlings could feed on their blood. No one knows where this entirely baseless story originated, but on the strength of the old fable, the pelican was frequently adopted as a Christian symbol of selfless love. Actually, of course, pelicans feed their young with the fish they are so adept at catching. They nest in colonies on the ground, usually on islands.

The brown pelican is considered the Louisiana state bird, although the choice has not been officially confirmed.

MAINE

Pine Cone and Tassel 1925 • Chickadee 1927

The only one among the fifty states that selected as its floral emblem not a flower in the usual sense of the word, Maine chose the pine cone and tassel as early as 1894 under the direction of the Maine Floral Emblem Society. Among the reasons was the fact that pine forests are one of Maine's great natural resources, and also that the tree has figured prominently in New England history ever since colonial days.

In 1925, the state legislature confirmed the choice made more than thirty years before by officially designating the pine cone and tassel as Maine's floral emblem.

58

It is not surprising that two northeastern states selected the lively, likable chickadee as their emblem. The Maine legislature adopted the common black-capped chickadee as the state bird in 1927.

Members of the titmouse group, chickadees are easily recognized. All are small, rather plump acrobats that can often be seen feeding while hanging upside down from a branch. During wintertime, they like to visit bird feeders, especially if suet mixed with grain is provided.

Their call is their name, and the clear *chick-adee-dee-dee* is one of the most cheerful outdoor sounds during the cold season. Chickadees are cavity nesters, and build their fur-lined nests in holes in old stumps or dead trees.

MARYLAND

Black-eyed Susan 1918 • Baltimore Oriole 1947

Also known as the yellow daisy, the black-eyed Susan is one of the many different kinds of coneflowers—some ninety species in all—that grow abundantly in fields, along roadsides, and in sandy soil over much of the eastern and central parts of the United States. The flowers, most of which are yellow, are distinguished by more or less cone-shaped, usually dark brown centers. Coneflowers vary from two to ten feet in height. The black-eyed Susan grows about three feet tall, has large golden flowerheads, and purplish-brown centers.

By act of the Maryland legislature, the black-eyed Susan was adopted as the state flower in 1918.

The striking golden orange-and-black coloration displayed throughout the year by the male Baltimore oriole is a reminder of this bird's tropical origin, which is further betayed by its preference for juicy fruits such as oranges. Most members of this group live south of our borders in Mexico, Central, and South America.

The Baltimore oriole's song is a series of rich, piping, often flutelike notes. Halved oranges wedged among sparsely leaved branches in the spring often attract orioles. At the same time, the much duller-colored female can be seen foraging for any loose piece of string or thread she can use to weave into her baglike nest, which is suspended from the outer branches of elm and other shade trees. The Baltimore oriole was designated as Maryland's state bird in 1947.

MASSACHUSETTS

Mayflower 1918 • Chickadee 1941

More accurately known as the trailing arbutus, the mayflower is cherished as one of the earliest spring flowers
in the Northeast. The plant, which belongs in the heath
family, has tough, hairy, evergreen leaves and fragrant
pink or white flowers. There is only a single species, which
formerly was common in sandy soils and rocky woodland
areas of the East, but has become scarce through over-
picking. For that reason, the law adopting the arbutus
as Massachusetts' state flower in 1918 was amended in
1925 by adding a paragraph designed to protect the
plant, and setting fines for digging up arbutus on public
land—or on private land without express consent of the
owner.

Massachusetts adopted the chickadee as its state bird in 1941, one of two northeastern states to select this lively and likable bird.

Members of the titmouse group, chickadees are easily recognized. All are small, rather plump acrobats that can often be seen feeding while hanging upside down from a branch. During wintertime, they like to visit bird feeders, especially if suet mixed with grain is provided.

Their call is their name, and the clear *chick-adee-dee-dee* is one of the most cheerful outdoor sounds during the cold season. Chickadees are cavity nesters, and build their fur-lined nests in holes in old stumps or dead trees.

MICHIGAN

Apple Blossom 1897 • Robin 1931

Declaring that "blossoming apple trees add much to the beauty" of Michigan's landscape, the state legislature adopted the apple blossom as its floral emblem in 1897, thereby making Michigan the first of two states to pay this tribute to one of the world's oldest and most famous fruit trees.

There are probably few other sights better suited to bring to mind so vividly the feeling of spring in temperate zones as the spectacle of an apple orchard in full bloom. As bees hum about in the scented air, the branches with their tightly packed, delicate pink-and-white blossoms provide not only beauty for the eye, but also the promise of a rich harvest of delicious fruit later on in the year.

One of three states to choose the robin as its state bird, Michigan so designated this "best known and best

64

loved of all birds in the state of Michigan" in 1931 by a resolution of its legislature.

Welcomed as the unerring harbinger of spring in many parts of the United States, the robin is a cheerful, friendly bird whose pleasant song enlivens many a suburban backyard and garden. It builds its mud-walled, grass-lined nest in a tree often close to human habitations.

The American robin was so named by homesick English settlers because it reminded them of the gentle "Robin Redbreast" of their homeland. The European robin, however, is a much smaller, warblerlike bird not closely related to the American species, which is a true thrush.

MINNESOTA

Moccasin Flower 1902 • Common Loon 1961

One of the most handsome of all the orchids in the more northern parts of our country, the showy lady's slipper, popularly known as the moccasin flower, displays its large pink-and-white blossoms against the shiny bright green of its leaves on the forest floor. North America has a dozen species of lady's slippers, of which the pink, the showy, and the yellow lady's slippers are the most widely known.

The Minnesota state legislature had actually selected the yellow lady's slipper as state flower in 1893, but when it was later shown that this particular species did not occur in Minnesota, the designation was changed to the pink-and-white showy lady's slipper in 1902.

The haunting cries of the common loon are among the most distinctive and enchanting sounds of the northern wildernesses. This vocal courtship performance of the male may resemble the howling of a wolf one minute, and then trail off into a series of yodeling, laughing notes that reverberate through the night.

There are only four species of loons in the world, and all four occur in the United States. The common loon's striking black-and-white pattern changes to plain gray above and white below during the winter months. Nests are built of a mass of debris piled up on an islet, or atop a muskrat house, or along the grassy edge of a freshwater lake or pond. The common loon was confirmed as the Minnesota state bird in 1961.

MISSISSIPPI

Magnolia 1900 • Mockingbird 1929

The schoolchildren of Mississippi in 1900 selected the evergreen magnolia, *Magnolia grandiflora*, by a margin of three to one over the cotton blossom, the runner-up, as the winning candidate for a state flower of Mississippi. The large, fragrant, white or pink magnolia blossom, which personifies the atmosphere and legendary charm of the Old South, is the floral emblem of two states.

Magnolias were named after French botanist Pierre Magnol (1638-1715). They comprise a group of trees and shrubs with large, showy blossoms that may range in color from white to pink and purple.

One of five states that chose the all-time favorite

among American songbirds, Mississippi officially designated the mockingbird as its emblem in 1929.

Famed as an accomplished vocalist, the mockingbird is unique in that its repertoire includes a great many songs of other birds in often perfect imitations, and also various notes, sounds, and noises picked up from its environment.

Mockingbirds occur throughout the entire southern half of the country, but are most numerous in the South and Southwest. They like to stay around human habitations and often build their rootlet-lined cup of a nest in gardens near houses. Not the least bit shy, they like to tease the family dog or cat.

MISSOURI

Hawthorn 1923 • Bluebird 1927

Hawthorns are a group of spring-flowering, spiny shrubs belonging to the apple family. Their small, fragrant flowers are white or pink, and they have glossy leaves and red, berrylike fruit called *haws*. The downy hawthorn, which is Missouri's floral emblem, is also known as "red haw," the color referring to the fruit.

Hawthorns are often planted as ornamental shrubs in Europe as well as in this country. The plant is used pharamaceutically to produce a heart drug. In adopting the hawthorn as state flower in 1923, the General Assembly of Missouri urged "the cultivation of said tree on account of the beauty of its flower, fruit, and foliage."

By designating it as the state bird in 1927, Missouri's General Assembly acknowledged the bluebird to be an overwhelming favorite of their citizens. One of the most attractive of our smaller thrushes, the bluebird is the emblem of two states.

Bluebirds are much more rarely seen today than they were years ago, but they still occur over much of the country. The eastern and western varieties are very similar and differ only in small details of appearance.

These cavity nesters will frequently accept bird boxes as nesting sites, especially on farms, because of the birds' preference for open countryside. According to old tradition, good fortune will come to those lucky enough to have a pair of these gentle birds nesting on their property.

MONTANA

Bitterroot 1895 • Western Meadowlark 1931

The bitterroot is a succulent plant of the Rocky Mountains, and is distinguished by handsome, showy, pink flowers, and by thick, mealy roots. It belongs to a predominantly tropical group of plants that includes the familiar purslane—whose leaves are used as pot herbs or for salads—and the spring beauties with their delicate pink flowers that are among the earliest blossoms to appear in the springtime.

In 1895, the bitterroot was officially adopted as Montana's floral emblem by an act of its state legislature.

In 1930, the schoolchildren of Montana voted for the meadowlark as the state bird and, in 1931, the legislature confirmed that choice. Six states in all have selected this common and attractive bird of the open prairies.

The meadowlark's song is clear and pleasant, but that of the western species is much more musical than that of the otherwise very similar eastern kind.

Members of the blackbird and oriole group, and not closely related to the true larks, meadowlarks are cherished because of their beauty, their song, and their value as checks on pest insects. The seeds they also eat are largely from noncultivated grasses and weeds. The nest is a grassy, partially domed cup built on the ground.

NEBRASKA

Goldenrod 1895 • Western Meadowlark 1929

One of the first states to select a floral emblem, Nebraska chose the goldenrod species *Solidago serotina*, often called the late goldenrod, in 1895. Two states have selected this wildflower, which is abundant throughout the country.

Of the more than 120 kinds of goldenrod in the United States, a few have pale yellow or even white flowers, but the great majority display the typical golden yellow that gave the plants their name.

Goldenrods bloom from summer to fall, and may line roadsides or carpet acres of meadows with a sheet of bright golden color. A few species have adapted to life in marshes, sandy beaches, deserts, and mountains.

In 1929, the meadowlark was confirmed as Nebraska's state bird by legislative act, which stated that the choice was based on a preference voiced by women's clubs, schoolchildren, and the Ornithologists' Union. Nebraska thus became one of six states to adopt this common and attractive bird of the open prairies.

The meadowlark's song is clear and pleasant, but that of the western species is much more musical than that of the otherwise very similar eastern kind.

Members of the blackbird and oriole group, and not closely related to the true larks, meadowlarks are cherished because of their beauty, their song, and their value as checks on pest insects. The seeds they also eat are largely from noncultivated grasses and weeds. The nest is a grassy, partially domed cup built on the ground.

NEVADA

Sagebrush 1917 • Mountain Bluebird 1967

The flower of the sagebrush is an appropriate choice for a western state, since this hardy, widespread plant of the western alkaline plains ranks among the most characteristic vegetation of that area. The sagelike odor of the leaves is responsible for the undershrub's popular name, yet it is not closely related to the mint of that name used to flavor meats and other foods.

Grayish-green leaves and small yellow flowers distinguish the sagebrush. It was adopted as the state floral emblem by the Nevada Senate in 1917, with the Assembly concurring.

76

The overwhelming choice of women's clubs, school-children, and other citizens of the state, the mountain bluebird was designated as Nevada's emblem in 1967, thereby becoming the declared favorite of two states.

The bluebird of the western mountain ranges lacks the rust-colored breast of its close relative, the common bluebird of the East and West. Instead, this small thrush is overall turquoise blue, somewhat paler below, and with a whitish belly. Its song is a short, clear warble.

Open terrain with scattered trees is the mountain bluebird's preferred environment, but it sometimes will live around farms, very much like its relatives. Also like other bluebirds, it is a cavity nester, and may be willing to accept a bird box as a substitute for the hole in a dead tree or stump in which it normally would build its nest.

NEW HAMPSHIRE

Lilac 1919 • *Purple Finch 1957*

Widely used in Europe as ornamental plants, and introduced at an early date into this country by English settlers, lilacs must be counted among the most beloved of flowering shrubs. In spring, the bushes with their pyramid-shaped clusters of small fragrant flowers are a common sight.

Selective breeding has produced lilacs with deep purplish and even white flowers, but the word "lilac" most commonly brings to mind a bluish-red or bluish-pink, lavender color. The name comes from the Arab word *laylak*, which in turn was adapted from the Persian

78

nilac, meaning bluish. The lilac was designated as the New Hampshire state flower in 1919.

Before they were driven out by the tough, garrulous house sparrow—which is a species introduced from Europe, and not closely related to our native sparrows— purple finches were much more common in the northeastern part of our country than they are today. The male of this sparrow-sized finch has been described as a "sparrow dipped in strawberry juice." The female is brownish and looks like a sparrow.

Purple finches prefer pine woods. Their nest, which is a shallow cup, is most often built in a coniferous tree. These birds usually travel in flocks, and are attracted to bird feeders in wintertime. Selected in 1927 by the New Hampshire women's clubs as their choice for the state bird, the purple finch was so designated officially in 1957.

NEW JERSEY

Violet 1913 • American Goldfinch 1935

By a concurring resolution of New Jersey's legislative bodies in 1913, the violet was selected as the state flower, partly because of its blue color, which designates hope, and partly because it is so common throughout the state. New Jersey thus is one of four states to select as their floral emblem one of the best known and best loved of all small wildflowers.

Long the symbol of modesty and shyness, violets are widely distributed in both the Old and New Worlds. Of the more than 300 species found worldwide, about 100 occur in the United States. In addition to the familiar blue violets, there are white and even yellow-flowered kinds. The latter include the downy yellow violet, which may grow to a height of eighteen inches, making it one of the tallest members of the entire group.

New Jersey's legislative assemblies adopted the American goldfinch—also known as the common or eastern goldfinch—in 1935. Two states chose this bird whose male, in its breeding plumage, is one of our most attractive smaller birds.

During wintertime, both males and females wear a rather drab grayish-green feather dress, but in spring the males change to bright yellow set off by black wings and tail, and a black forehead.

These birds live in open, weedy fields and travel in flocks. They often can be seen clinging to the stem of a tall weed or grass while picking off the seeds. The nest is a tightly woven feltlike cup placed in a bush or tree.

NEW MEXICO

Yucca Flower 1927 • Roadrunner 1949

The unique yuccas of the arid regions of the American Southwest are related to the lily and palm families. They range from plants only a few feet tall to the huge, treelike giant yuccas known as Joshua trees, which bear their pineapple-shaped flower clusters on branched arms. Yuccas are noted for their interdependent relationship with the small white yucca moths, without which the flowers could not be pollinated. In exchange, the yucca provides part of its seeds as food for the developing moth larvae, a striking example of the give-and-take principle found often in nature.

Chosen by women's clubs and schoolchildren, the yucca was confirmed as New Mexico's floral emblem in 1927 by legislative action.

No other bird is as typical of the arid southwestern regions as the peculiar roadrunner, the cuckoo that can fly but prefers to run. For its size, the brownish, heavily streaked roadrunner is a formidable predator. In addition to large insects, it will kill and eat any lizard, snake, or other animal it can overpower. Small reptiles make up a large part of this bird's diet. The nest is a shallow cup in low trees, bushes, or cactus plants. Unlike some of its relatives, the roadrunner is not a brood parasite and takes care of its own young.

After emerging as the front-runner for choice as New Mexico's state bird, the roadrunner was officially designated in 1949.

NEW YORK

Wild Rose 1891 • Bluebird 1970

When the state's schoolchildren selected the wild rose as the floral emblem on Arbor Day, 1891, New York became the first of three states to choose that perennial favorite of poets and songwriters as the state flower.

The fragrant, delicate pink or white blossoms of these rambling shrubs long ago captured the affection and imagination of people in many countries. Roses probably were among the earliest of cultivated flowers, and are mentioned in some very ancient literature. As noted in the introduction, the rose was in the past considered a symbol of discretion and secrecy, and frequently used as an emblem.

A campaign to select a state bird by New York women's clubs in 1927-28 showed the bluebird to be the leading favorite, yet it was not officially adopted until 1970. This beautiful small thrush thus is the emblem of two of our states.

Bluebirds are much more rarely seen today than they were years ago, but they still occur over much of the country. The eastern and western varieties are very similar and differ only in small details of appearance.

These cavity nesters will frequently accept bird boxes as nesting sites, especially on farms, because of the birds' preference for open countryside. According to old tradition, good fortune will come to those lucky enough to have a pair of these gentle birds nesting on their property.

NORTH CAROLINA

Flowering Dogwood 1941 • Cardinal 1943

By changing its floral emblem from the oxeye daisy to the flowering dogwood in 1941, North Carolina was the second state to adopt what surely is one of the most beautiful of American flowering trees.

In spring, the foliage all but disappears under the masses of large, pink or white blossoms. Actually, what look like four large petals really are the outer leaves, or bracts, that in most flowers are green and enclose the colored petals while they are still in the bud. The dogwood's true flowers are small, greenish, and clustered in the center.

By choosing the cardinal as the state bird in 1943, North Carolina became one of seven states that have declared this their favorite bird.

86

Easily identified because both the bright red male and the duller, brownish female wear crests, the cardinal is further distinguished by the fact that the male keeps its colorful plumage throughout the entire year.

In wintertime, when snow is on the ground, cardinals provide flashes of brilliant scarlet as they visit bird feeders for their favorite sunflower seeds. Originally a bird of river thickets and woodland edges, the cardinal has adapted well to man's presence, and now makes its home in suburban areas and even in towns, where it is a welcome guest. Its nest is a loose cup built in a bush or thicket.

NORTH DAKOTA

Wild Rose 1907 • Western Meadowlark 1947

The third state to choose that perennial favorite of poets and songwriters, North Dakota designated the wild rose —or, more exactly, the variety known as wild prairie rose —as its floral emblem in 1907.

The fragrant, delicate pink or white blossoms of these rambling shrubs long ago captured the affection and imagination of people in many countries. Roses probably were among the earliest of cultivated flowers, and are mentioned in some very ancient literature. As noted in the introduction, the rose was in the past considered a symbol of discretion and secrecy, and frequently used as an emblem.

North Dakota, in 1947, became one of six states that declared their affection for the meadowlark by choosing this common and attractive bird of the open prairies as their state bird.

The meadowlark's song is clear and pleasant, but that of the western species is much more musical than that of the otherwise very similar eastern kind.

Members of the blackbird and oriole group, and not closely related to the true larks, meadowlarks are cherished because of their beauty, their song, and their value as checks on pest insects. The seeds they also eat are largely from noncultivated grasses and weeds. The nest is a grassy, partially domed cup built on the ground.

OHIO

Scarlet Carnation 1904 • Cardinal 1933

Carnations are cultivated varieties of the clove pink, a wildflower distinguished by its rich clovelike fragrance. They are counted among the best-loved of all garden flowers. Along with such varieties of the clove pink as the china and garden pinks, the double-flowered carnations in white, pink, and scarlet are the pride of many gardens.

In selecting the scarlet carnation as its state flower, the Ohio legislature in 1904 expressly stated that this flower was the favorite of one famous citizen of Ohio, and that it therefore was chosen "as a token of love and reverence for the memory of William McKinley."

Ohio was one of the seven states that proclaimed

90

their preference for the handsome cardinal by designating it as Ohio's state bird in 1933.

Easily identified because both the bright red male and the duller, brownish female wear crests, the cardinal is further distinguished by the fact that the male keeps its colorful plumage throughout the entire year.

In wintertime, when snow is on the ground, cardinals provide flashes of brilliant scarlet as they visit bird feeders for their favorite sunflower seeds. Originally a bird of river thickets and woodland edges, the cardinal has adapted well to man's presence, and now makes its home in suburban areas and even in towns, where it is a welcome guest. Its nest is a loose cup built in a bush or thicket.

OKLAHOMA

Mistletoe 1893 • Scissor-tailed Flycatcher 1951

The legendary mistletoe of Europe is a parasitic green shrub, and was one of the plants singled out for veneration by the ancient Celts. It is still widely used in England today for Christmas decorations, with the attendant custom that any man may kiss the girl of his choice while standing under a branch of mistletoe. The American variety is a related plant that lives on certain deciduous trees, from which it gets its food.

Mistletoes have small yellow flowers and waxy, pearl-like white berries. In 1893, the Territorial legislature of Oklahoma adopted the mistletoe as its floral emblem.

92

One of the most beautiful and graceful of our smaller native birds, the scissor-tailed flycatcher inhabits certain western parts of the United States. It is frequently seen

in those regions along roadsides and on farms and ranches, generally preferring semi-open country, including areas covered with mesquite and similar vegetation.

Although a member of the kingbird family, this small pearly-gray bird with its pink-flushed underside is set apart from its relatives by the unique, scissor-shaped tail that makes up fully two-thirds of its overall length. The nest is a shallow cup of grass and twigs in a bush, tree, or even atop a telephone pole. In 1951, the scissor-tailed flycatcher was adopted as Oklahoma's state bird.

OREGON

Oregon Grape 1899 • Western Meadowlark 1927

The attractive evergreen shrub known as the Oregon grape occurs widely in both Oregon and California, and is frequently used as an ornamental plant in parks and gardens of both states. Despite its name, the Oregon grape is not related to the familiar grapevines, being instead a member of the barberry family. The flowers of this shrub are small and yellowish. The dark blue berries, which resemble small grapes, are responsible for the popular name.

In 1899, the legislative Assembly of Oregon designated the Oregon grape as the state's floral emblem.

One of the six states to select the meadowlark as their

state bird, Oregon made its choice of this common and attractive bird of the open prairies in 1927 by popular vote of its schoolchildren. In the same year, the governor confirmed it by issuing a proclamation.

The meadowlark's song is clear and pleasant, but that of the western species is much more musical than that of the otherwise very similar eastern kind.

Members of the blackbird and oriole group, and not closely related to the true larks, meadowlarks are cherished because of their beauty, their song, and their value as checks on pest insects. The seeds they also eat are largely from noncultivated grasses and weeds. The nest is a grassy, partially domed cup built on the ground.

PENNSYLVANIA

Mountain Laurel 1933 • Ruffed Grouse 1931

Adopted by two eastern states as their floral emblem, this handsome evergreen American shrub is not closely related to the European true laurel of ancient fame. A member of the azalea and rhododendron group, the mountain laurel brings forth its beautiful clusters of small, rose-colored or pinkish-white flowers in late spring. The leaves of this evergreen plant are poisonous when eaten.

In 1933, the mountain laurel, which grows abundantly in many parts of the state, was adopted as the floral emblem of Pennsylvania by an act of the General Assembly.

The ruffed grouse probably ranks as the number one favorite among all the game birds of the United States. This small grouse—which is monogamous, in contrast to many other members of its group— prefers open woodlands and broken scrub country. In the spring, the famous drumming sounds made by the courting male while perching on a log are familiar to anyone who has ever visited grouse country during the mating season. This loud drumming noise is produced solely by the grouse's cupped wings beating rapidly against air.

The ruffed grouse nests on the ground, usually in a sheltered depression on the forest floor. In 1931, Pennsylvania declared this grouse to be the state bird by an act of the legislature.

RHODE ISLAND

Violet 1897 • Rhode Island Red 1954

The first of the four states to choose the violet as its floral emblem, Rhode Island adopted it in 1897 after the state's schoolchildren had voted overwhelmingly for this much-loved small wildflower.

Long the symbol of modesty and shyness, violets are widely distributed in both the Old and New Worlds. Of the more than 300 species found worldwide, about 100 occur in the United States. In addition to the familiar blue violets, there are white and even yellow-flowered kinds. The latter include the downy yellow violet, which may grow to a height of eighteen inches, making it one of the tallest members of the entire group.

The decision to chose as its state bird the breed of domestic fowl that carries Rhode Island's name was based mainly on its economic importance. Internationally known as a fine American breed of barnyard fowl, the Rhode Island Red is distinguished from other varieties by the rich, solid chestnut brown of its plumage. Although most people never pause to think about it, our domestic fowl are true pheasants. All of them were bred from wild Asiatic ancestors—probably the Red Jungle fowl of India—and still betray their pheasant origin in the roosters' enlarged and iridescent tail feathers.

The Rhode Island Red was designated as Rhode Island's state bird in 1954.

SOUTH CAROLINA

Carolina Jessamine 1924 • Carolina Wren 1943

The sweet-scented yellow flowers of the Carolina jessamine—often also called yellow jasmine—make this climbing plant a great favorite as an ornamental in gardens and around houses in southern states. It is not closely related to the famed white jasmine of poetry, which belongs in the olive family.

The name of these plants comes from the Arabic *yasamin*, which in turn was adapted from the Persian *yasaman*. Under its scientific name of *Gelsemium*, the root of the yellow jasmine is used in pharmaceutics. After an appointed commission had selected the Carolina jessamine as South Carolina's floral emblem in 1923, the General Assembly officially confirmed the choice in 1924.

100

One of the larger of our native wrens, the Carolina wren is a rust-colored species found primarily in the southeastern part of the country, where it displays all the cheerful activity generally associated with the wren group.

Although the Carolina wren likes to live in thickets and streamside undergrowth, it is not at all shy, and does not shun human habitations. Like other wrens, it frequently accepts bird boxes as a convenient place to build its nest and raise its family. After the Carolina women's clubs had selected the Carolina wren as their candidate for state bird in 1931, it was officially so designated in 1943.

SOUTH DAKOTA

Pasqueflower 1903 • Ring-necked Pheasant 1948

The purple, violet, or sometimes white blossoms of this plant are familiar sights in the prairie regions of the Midwest during springtime. The name, which comes from the old French, means Easterflower. The plant is a member of the crowfoot family and allied to the buttercups. Its seeds have long, silky, feathery tails which permit them to be easily spread by the wind.

In 1903, the pasqueflower was adopted as the floral

emblem of South Dakota, the reason being in part that it is one of the first flowers to bloom on the prairies.

Although originally hailing from Asia like the rest of its family, the ring-necked pheasant has been successfully introduced into many countries, including our own, and has established itself without difficulty in these new environments. A favored game bird, its preferred habitat is irrigated land, including farmland. The nest is a grass-lined hollow among tall grasses.

Phasianus colchicus, the pheasant's scientific name, serves as a reminder that this handsomely colored, iridescent bird was known to the ancient Greeks as hailing from the land they called Colchis, a location identified as coinciding with the region which today comprises Russian Georgia on the Black Sea. The ring-necked pheasant was designated as South Dakota's state bird in 1948.

TENNESSEE

Iris 1933 • Mockingbird 1933

The common iris, also called the blue flag, is undoubtedly one of the most handsome and showy wildflowers in the United States. Many different varieties of iris grow in moist but open locations, such as wet weadows, through-out the world's temperate regions. The varicolored hues displayed by iris flowers account for the plant's name, which means "rainbow." Many wild and cultivated varieties are great garden favorites.

In 1933, Tennessee adopted the iris as its state flower by a Senate joint resolution, thereby repealing the law that had made the passion flower the state's floral emblem after schoolchildren selected it in 1919.

Also in 1933, the mockingbird was designated as Tennessee's state bird, making it the last of the five states to choose this favorite among American songbirds.

Famed as an accomplished vocalist, the mockingbird is unique in that its repertoire includes a great many songs of other birds in often perfect imitations, and also various notes, sounds, and noises picked up from its environment.

Mockingbirds occur throughout the entire southern half of the country, but are most numerous in the South and Southwest. They like to stay around human habitations and often build their rootlet-lined cup of a nest in gardens near houses. Not the least bit shy, they like to tease the family dog or cat.

TEXAS

Bluebonnet 1901 • Mockingbird 1927

Locally known as "buffalo clover," the bluebonnet is one of the approximately 150 species of lupines found in this country. All but one are confined to the western half of the United States. The pea-type flowers may come in blue, purple, pink, white, or yellow, depending upon the species. The plants are poisonous to cattle, but their seeds are valuable food for game birds.

By an act of legislature in 1901, Texas designated the bluebonnet as that state's floral emblem.

"A singer of a distinctive type; a fighter for the protection of his home, falling if need be, in its defense, like any true Texan." With these words, the Texas legislature

106

in 1927 adopted the mockingbird as the state bird, one of five states to choose this favorite among American songbirds.

Famed as an accomplished vocalist, the mockingbird is unique in that its repertoire includes a great many songs of other birds in often perfect imitations, and also various notes, sounds, and noises picked up from its environment.

Mockingbirds occur throughout the entire southern half of the country, but are most numerous in the South and Southwest. They like to stay around human habitations and often build their rootlet-lined cup of a nest in gardens near houses. Not the least bit shy, they like to tease the family dog or cat.

UTAH

Sego Lily 1911 • California Gull 1955

A graceful plant with slender stems, grasslike leaves, and tulip-shaped flowers, the sego lily is one of the mariposas, and is also known as the mariposa lily or tulip. A member of the lily family, not only in name but in fact, it is found exclusively in the West, where it may blanket desert foothills and other hillsides with its handsome white flowers in the spring.

The Indians in the past used the small edible bulbs as food, and so did the Mormons during the lean years between 1840 and 1850. Approval of the sego lily as Utah's floral emblem by an act of the legislature in 1911 was based as much on that old memory as on the beauty of the flower.

108

The California gull is a species often found in western inland lakes such as the Salton Sea of the Coachella Valley. The appearance of huge flocks of gulls near Salt Lake City in 1848 signaled the settlers' deliverance from the locust plague that had brought them to the edge of starvation. The sight of the white gulls gorging themselves on the blackish insects was likened by the religious pioneers to a fight between the "hosts of Heaven and Hell." When the gulls left, the pests were vanquished, and the people saved. A lovely statue of a gull was erected in Salt Lake City to commemorate that event, and in 1955 the grateful citizens of Utah, who had always considered the California gull their state bird, made their choice official.

VERMONT

Red Clover 1894 • Hermit Thrush 1941

The red clover is only one of some seventy-five species found in this country; about two-thirds of them occur in the West. Red, white, and Alsike clover enrich the soil, are excellent food for livestock, and provide us with some of our most delicious honey. In addition, the seeds of several western species are an important food for quail and other birds.

All things considered, it would be hard to find another wildflower that provides man with so many different advantages as this familiar and humble relative of the pea. The plant's usefulness to the farming industry of

Vermont was the prime reason for its adoption as the state's floral emblem by an act of the legislature in 1894.

Although it wears a plain brownish feather dress, the hermit thrush deserves a special place as one of our finest natural musicians. Its song has an ethereal, flutelike quality matched by few other birds.

This thrush is found widely over many parts of the United States, preferring underbrush in mixed woods, thickets, or parklands. It may sometimes be mistaken for a mouse as it scurries along among dead leaves and other debris in the underbrush, where it searches for worms and insects. The nest is a cup of grass, moss, and small roots built on the ground or in a low tree. The hermit thrush was designated as Vermont's state bird in 1941.

VIRGINIA

Flowering Dogwood 1918 • Cardinal 1950

The first of two states that chose the flowering dogwood as their floral emblem, Virginia so designated it in 1918 because, as noted in the act of the state legislature, the tree adds so much to the beauty of the Virginia landscape.

In spring, the foliage all but disappears under the masses of large, pink or white blossoms. Actually, what look like four large petals really are the outer leaves, or bracts, that in most flowers are green and enclose the colored petals while they are still in the bud. The dogwood's true flowers are small, greenish, and clustered in the center.

Because it cannot tolerate very cold temperatures, the dogwood is a tree mainly of the more southern parts of the country, where it often grows in abundance.

112

In 1950, Virginia joined the ranks of the seven states that adopted the cardinal as their state bird.

Easily identified because both the bright red male and the duller, brownish female wear crests, the cardinal is further distinguished by the fact that the male keeps its colorful plumage throughout the entire year.

In wintertime, when snow is on the ground, cardinals provide flashes of brilliant scarlet as they visit bird feeders for their favorite sunflower seeds. Originally a bird of river thickets and woodland edges, the cardinal has adapted well to man's presence, and now makes its home in suburban areas and even in towns, where it is a welcome guest. Its nest is a loose cup built in a bush or thicket.

WASHINGTON

Pink Rhododendron • *Willow Goldfinch 1951*

The western variety of rhododendron, often known as the California rhododendron, is one among many species of this group of mostly evergreen shrubs of the heath family. They are at home in the mountainous regions of the Northern Hemisphere, and have become favorite ornamentals for parks and gardens. Their handsome flowers come in a variety of colors ranging from pure white over lavender to pink and purple.

Although there seems to be nothing in the records to say when it was adopted as Washington's floral emblem, it was selected by the people because "it blooms in all its beauty here," according to a librarian in the Washington State Library.

114

A western subspecies of the American, or eastern, goldfinch, the willow goldfinch is found only along the Pacific coast from Oregon to Southern California. The paler, more olive-hued yellow which the male wears even during the breeding season makes it a much less conspicuous bird than its eastern relative.

As its name implies, the willow goldfinch prefers a habitat of willow bushes growing in clumps streamside or in marshy places. The nest is a small, feltlike cup in a small tree or bush. The willow goldfinch was designated as Washington's state bird in 1951.

WEST VIRGINIA

Great Rhododendron 1903 • Cardinal 1949

Locally known as the big laurel, this large-leaved rhododendron with its showy, usually pink flowers is the common species of the eastern United States, and grows to a considerable size. It is often seen in parks and showcase gardens in and around eastern cities, and is a magnificent sight when in full bloom. The large, tubular flowers may attract sphinx moths as well as hummingbirds searching for nectar.

In 1903, the great rhododendron was adopted as the state floral emblem by the West Virginia General Assembly, thereby confirming the choice made in 1902 by the state's schoolchildren.

By selecting the cardinal as its state bird in 1949,

West Virginia became one of seven states that preferred the "red bird" above all others.

Easily identified because both the bright red male and the duller, brownish female wear crests, the cardinal is further distinguished by the fact that the male keeps its colorful plumage throughout the entire year.

In wintertime, when snow is on the ground, cardinals provide flashes of brilliant scarlet as they visit bird feeders for their favorite sunflower seeds. Originally a bird of river thickets and woodland edges, the cardinal has adapted well to man's presence, and now makes its home in suburban areas and even in towns, where it is a welcome guest. Its nest is a loose cup built in a bush or thicket.

WISCONSIN

Violet 1908 • Robin 1926

By a vote of the state's schoolchildren, Wisconsin selected the violet as its floral emblem in 1908, thereby becoming one of the four states to choose that much-loved small wildflower.

Long the symbol of modesty and shyness, violets are widely distributed in both the Old and New Worlds. Of the more than 300 species found worldwide, about 100 occur in the United States. In addition to the familiar blue violets, there are white and even yellow-flowered kinds. The latter include the downy yellow violet, which may grow to a height of eighteen inches, making it one of the tallest members of the entire group.

First of the three states to confirm the robin as their state bird, Wisconsin adopted it in 1926 after school-children had chosen it in a statewide vote.

Welcomed as the unerring harbinger of spring in many parts of the United States, the robin is a cheerful, friendly bird whose pleasant song enlivens many a sub-urban backyard and garden. It builds its mud-walled, grass-lined nest in a tree often close to human habitations.

The American robin was so named by homesick English settlers because it reminded them of the gentle "Robin Redbreast" of their homeland. The European robin, however, is a much smaller, warblerlike bird not closely related to the American species, which is a true thrush.

WYOMING

Painted Cup 1917 • Western Meadowlark 1927

The members of the figwort family known as painted cups or Indian paintbrushes are common and attractive wildflowers of western prairies and hillsides. The actual flowers are small and inconspicuous. The brilliant color that identifies these plants when in bloom is located in the bracts, the leaves that surround and enclose the flower while it is still a bud. Most of the thirty-five species of painted cups have red flowers. Some, however, are red and yellow, and a few, just yellow.

By an act of the Wyoming legislature, the state adopted a common red species of Indian paintbrush as its floral emblem in 1917.

One of the first of six states to select the western

120

meadowlark as their state bird, Wyoming made the choice in 1927. Although the legislature specified only "the meadowlark," the bird found in Wyoming is the western species of this common and attractive bird of the open prairies.

The meadowlark's song is clear and pleasant, but that of the western species is much more musical than that of the otherwise very similar eastern kind.

Members of the blackbird and oriole group, and not closely related to the true larks, meadowlarks are cherished because of their beauty, their song, and their value as checks on pest insects. The seeds they also eat are largely from noncultivated grasses and weeds. The nest is a grassy, partially domed cup built on the ground.

List of Scientific Names

FLOWERS

Apple, *Malus* sp.
Arbutus, trailing, *Epigaea repens*
Bitterroot, *Lewisia rediviva*
Black-eyed Susan, *Rudbeckia hirta*
Bluebonnet, *Lupinus subcarnosis*
Camellia, *Thea japonica*
Carnation, *Dianthus* sp.
Clove pink, *Dianthus caryophyllus*
Clover, red, *Trifolium pratense*
Columbine, blue, *Aquilegia coerulea*
Dogwood, flowering, *Cynoxylon floridum*
Forget-me-not, alpine, *Myosotis alpestris*
           common, *Myosotis palustris*
Goldenrod, *Solidago* sp.
Hawthorn, downy, *Crataegus mollis*
Iris, common, *Iris versicolor*
Jessamine, Carolina, *Gelsemium sempervirens*
Lady's slipper, showy, *Cypropedium reginae*
Laurel, European, *Laurus nobilis*
      mountain, *Kalmia latifolia*
Lilac, *Syringa vulgaris*
Lily, Madonna, *Lilium candidum*
      sego, *Calochortus nuttallii*
Magnolia, evergreen, *Magnolia grandiflora*
Mariposa, *Calochortus* sp.
Mistletoe, American, *Phoradendron flavescens*
      European, *Viscum album*
Moccasin flower. *See* Lady's slipper
Mountain laurel. *See* Laurel

123

Olive, *Olea europaea*
Orange, *Citrus sinensis*
Oregon grape, *Mahonia arguifolia*
Painted cup, *Castilleja linariaefolia*
Pasqueflower, *Pulsatilla ludoviciana*
Peach, *Amydalus persica*
Pine, *Pinus* sp.
Poppy, California, *Eschscholtzia californica*
       opium, *Papaver somniferus*
Rhododendron, great, *Rhododendron maximum*
             pink (western), *Rhododendron californicum*
Rose, *Rosa* sp.
    Cherokee, *Rosa laevigata*
    wild prairie, *Rosa segiris*
Sagebrush, *Artemisia tridentata*
Saguaro cactus, *Carnegiea gigantea*
Sunflower, common, *Helianthus annuus*
Syringa, *Philadelphus lewisii*
Violet, *Viola* sp.
Yucca, *Yucca* sp.

BIRDS

"Blue hen chicken," *Gallus gallus* var.
Bluebird, common, *Sialis sialis*
      mountain, *Sialis currocoides*
Bunting, lark, *Calamospiza menalocorys*
Cardinal, *Richmondena cardinalis*
Chickadee, black-capped, *Penthestes atricapillus*
Dove, rock, *Columba livia*
Eagle, bald, *Haliaeetus leucocephalus*
     golden, *Aquila chrysaetos*
     sea, *Haliaeetus* sp.
Finch, purple, *Carpodacus purpureus*
Flicker, yellow-shafted, *Colaptes auratus*
Flycatcher, scissor-tailed, *Muscivora forficata*
Goldfinch, American, *Spinus tristis*
      willow, *Spinus tristis salicamans*
Grouse, ruffed, *Bonasa umbellus*
Gull, California, *Larus californicus*
Ibis, sacred, *Threskiornis aethiopica*
Kiwi, *Apteryx australis*
Loon, common, *Agavia immer*
Meadowlark, western, *Sturnella neglecta*

Mockingbird, *Mimus polyglottos*
Nene (Hawaiian goose), *Branta sandvicensis*
Oriole, Baltimore, *Icterus galbula*
Pelican, brown, *Pelecanus occidentalis*
Pheasant, ring-necked, *Phasianus colchicus*
Ptarmigan, rock, *Lagopus mutus*
        white-tailed, *Lagopus leucurus*
        willow, *Lagopus lagopus*
Quail, California, *Lophortyx californicus*
Quetzal, *Pharomacrus moccino*
Red, Rhode Island, *Gallus gallus* var.
Roadrunner, *Geococcyx californianus*
Robin, American, *Turdus migratorius*
Thrasher, brown, *Toxostoma rufum*
Thrush, hermit, *Hylocichla guttata*
Turkey, *Meleagris gallopavo*
Wren, cactus, *Campylorhynchus brunneicapillum*
        Carolina, *Thryothorus ludovicianus*

Index